Prayer Kids

Modern prayers for children today

Rosemary and Peter Atkins
with illustrations by
Olivia Jackson-Mee

VERITAS

Prayer Kids was first published in 2007 by St Aidan's Parish, Remuera, Auckland, New Zealand for distribution in New Zealand and Australia. This edition is published by Veritas Publications of Dublin for the regions of the United Kingdom, Northern Ireland and the Republic of Ireland.

ISBN 978 1 84730 085 0
Published 2008 by
Veritas Publications
7/8 Lower Abbey Street
Dublin 1
Ireland
Email publications@veritas.ie
Website www.veritas.ie

Text © Rosemary and Peter Atkins, 2008
Illustrations © Olivia Jackson-Mee, 2008

All rights reserved. No part of this book may be reproduced in any form without written permission from the copyright holders. The authors can be contacted at 9a Paunui Street, St Heliers, Auckland 1005, New Zealand, by email at peter.rosemary@xtra.co.nz and by fax at 0064-9-5750477.

The material in this publication is protected by copyright law. Except as may be permitted by law, no part of the material may be reproduced (including by storage in a retrieval system) or transmitted in any form or by any means, adapted, rented or lent without the written permission of the copyright owners.

A catalogue record for this book is available from the British Library.

Designed by Barbara Croatto
Printed in the Republic of Ireland by Betaprint, Dublin

Veritas books are printed on paper made from the wood pulp of managed forests. For every tree felled, at least one tree is planted, thereby renewing natural resources.

Contents

My Prayers for Today

A new day dawns	1
Oh! it's raining	2
My team	2
When I am hungry	3
I like fizz	3
To smile and to dare	4
Sorry God, please forgive me	5
Other kids wear labels	5
I have homework to do	6
Why do big people always say 'No'?	7
Saying 'Yes' and saying 'No'	7
Wow, I made it!	8
Why was I not chosen?	8
Watch out for cars!	9
I like my friends	10
Jesus my friend	10
Dear God, what are manners?	11
I feel so special	12
Now it's bedtime	12

My Prayers for Others

For my family	13
For my grandparents	13
For .... who is in hospital	14
For my pet	15
For my school	15
For my church	16
For my country	16

My Prayers at Special Times

On my birthday	17
Hurray for holidays	18
Christmas is here again	18
Sadness and joy at Easter	20
First steps in faith	21
When I am sick	22
When someone I love has died	23
We were special friends	24
When I am hurt by others	25
Going away on my own	26
I feel uncomfortable	27
Squabbles in our family	28
Watching the family split up	29
Being part of a new family	30

About this book

Hi kids, this book has been put together to help you pray to God about all the things that mean most to you. PRAYER KIDS: Modern prayers for children today is the latest in a series of books of prayers to help young people and their families enter into a relationship with God through prayers in the language of today.

The authors of the series are Rosemary and Peter Atkins, who have long experience in providing prayer material in various books published worldwide. They both worship at St Aidan's Parish, Auckland, New Zealand, where Rosemary is a liturgical assistant and Peter is a retired Bishop. Olivia Jackson-Mee has contributed the illustrations, which give colour and interpretation to the prayers through the eyes of a young person.

Further information can be found on the website of the parish: www.staidans.co.nz

This book is dedicated to Meaghan and Caitlin,
our granddaughters,
(and their friend, Beanie).

MY PRAYERS FOR TODAY

A new day dawns

Creator God, thank you for this new day,
bless me,
    and my family,
        and my friends today,
especially .... who needs your help.

Help me to be kind today,
    to learn my lessons well,
        and to care for your creation.

May I be happy with friends who are happy
and care for those who are troubled or sad,
that with your strength
    I can serve you, my God,
        all this day.

Oh! It's raining

Oh! It's raining and our .... will be cancelled.

Creating God, I know that this is your world
      and some places need the rain.
Help me to be patient and to look forward
      to our fun in the sun on another day.

Your rainbow promises
      that you will always care for your world,
      balancing sunshine and rain,
            so 'Don't forget the violet' in the rainbow,
                and don't forget our special day too.

My team

Sweet! I'm in the .... team,
and we are going to be the best team in the world.

Jesus, I am sure you played sport
      when you were my age.
Teach me to play well and fairly,
      and to eat well and keep fit.
Help us to grow together as a team,
      supporting and
      encouraging one another.

      Bless our team today.

When I am hungry

Jesus, you went to school in your village of Nazareth.
When I go to school
      sometimes it is not long before I feel hungry.
Then I feel tired and cannot think or write very well.

Help me to say to my family
      that I need more food in the early morning
and if I don't have enough for breakfast,
      give me courage to tell my teacher
            why I find it hard to learn.
Jesus, I long to grow strong
            to serve you each day.

I like fizz

I like fizz – and biscuits – and takeaways too.
Grown-ups tell me that I will be unhealthy
      if I have too much of them.

Dear God, help me to listen to what they say
      and to eat the right foods,
so that I will keep well and strong
      and care for the body you have given me.

To smile and to dare

Beanie the bear has short brown hair
    and a smile that is always there.

Dear God,
    with the love he has brought me
        and the care he has taught me,
help me each day
    to love and to care
    to smile and to dare
        for that is your will for me.

Sorry God, please forgive me

Lord Jesus, I try to be good and to be like you,
but today I ……………

I am so sad and so sorry
    because I know you would not have said or done
    things like that.
Please forgive me, and give me strength
    to do it your way next time.

Other kids wear labels

Dear God, I am not quite sure why other kids
think it is important to have clothes with special labels.
Some of mine have labels too – but not all.
Labels or not, they are always clean
and as I put them on
    they smell so nice. (Thanks Mum!)
Help me to wear them well
    and look after my clothes.

Caring God I know you value me,
not for what I wear
    but for who I am.

I have homework to do

Wise God, there is so much to learn at school each day
    and I try to do my best.
But after school
    I am told to get on with my homework,
        when I just want to stop and play.

Help me to work out a plan with my family,
    with time to eat, time to study
        and time to relax.
Then I will be well prepared for school tomorrow
    and finally prepared for life in your world.

Why do big people always say 'No'?

'Don't touch!'; 'Don't do that!';
'Don't step off the pavement!';
'Don't leave your room in a mess!'
Don't, don't, don't – why don't they give me space to grow?

Dear God, help me to understand the dangers
    that they want me to avoid
and help them to understand
    that I must grow up to take responsibility for myself.

Saying 'Yes' and saying 'No'

No, no, no, no, no, NO!

Dear God, I only meant to say – no, no, NO!
And it is only because I want to help them understand
    that, NO, I am not a baby any more,
    and NO, I don't want to do that just now.

I want to be able to say, YES,
    I am grown-up enough to make some choices
    and act like your Son, Jesus, my friend.

Wow, I made it!

Lord Jesus, can you understand my joy and excitement?
I have had this success. I ....

Yes, you too knew real joy as the crowd cheered you
    on your ride into Jerusalem on Palm Sunday.

Help me to go on from here,
    joyful but humble in this success,
        thinking also of others
            and striving for new achievements
                on my journey through life.

Why was I not chosen?

Why was I not chosen? I would have done my very best.
I'm shattered. I really want to know WHY?
Jesus, you knew disappointment, so please
    calm me
        and help me understand.

Was I too young, or too small, or too big?
    Was it just not my day?
I am sure there was a reason
    and I will get my turn another time.
So help me to be patient, not to give up
and to work hard until it is my chance to shine.

Watch out for cars!

They tell me the drill:
    'Look right; look left; look right again'
and if nothing is coming,
    'Now cross the road, and walk and do not run'.

Dear God, keep me calm and safe.
It is hard to remember left from right
    and right from left,
        and to take time to look carefully.
            So help me to remember these rules
                and watch out for the traffic,
            so I will return safely to my home again.

I like my friends

Dear Jesus, I know you had friends when you lived on earth.
You walked and talked, and shared life together.
I guess you laughed and joked as well.

Thank you for my friends and the fun we have together.

Bless our times of sharing
      as we discover who we are
           and how we can help each other.

Jesus my friend

Jesus, you are my friend,
      and I know you love and care about me:
           about my health and happiness,
           about what I learn and what I acheive,
           about my friends
                  and the times we share together.

Be always near to guide me,
      to lead me into your ways
           and to increase my faith in you,
                my Lord and my friend.

Dear God, what are manners?

Dear God,
    what are MANNERS
and why do I get told
    'to mind your manners'?
I just don't understand why.

It seems to mean
    that I should think of others before myself.
        Now I remember,
            Jesus in the Bible taught his friends
                that they should put others first
            and love even those who hated them,
       so, if manners means that,
          I will follow Jesus
              and do things his way.

I feel so special

Thank you God that I am so special,
    because you made me,
        you love me
            and you gave me special gifts.
Please, dear God, care for me always.

Now it's bedtime

God of the day and God of the night,
thank you for all that has happened today
especially ….

Thank you for those who care for me
and bless us all this night.

May your Holy Angels watch over me
and keep me safe as I sleep.

MY PRAYERS FOR OTHERS

For my family

Dear God, bless our family.
Bless ...., ..., ... and ....

Help us to show love for one another
    with words and smiles,
    with understanding and forgiveness,
    and with actions to show we care.

Keep us loving, keep us loyal,
    keep us learning from one another.
Unite our family with your gift of love.

For my grandparents

Loving God, bless my grandparents.
Bless ...., ..., ... and ....,
and care for them as they grow older.

Help me to show my love
    and to be patient if they get a little tired.
Young and old, keep us firm in the bonds we share
    as they teach me lots and love me heaps.

For .... who is in hospital

.... has gone to hospital today.
Healing God, hospitals always seem strange
    but important places.
Though I miss .... I pray
that hospital is the place to make *her/him* well again.
Guide the doctors in their caring
    and help the nurses
        to be kind and comforting.

Dear God, may your healing spirit
    make .... better
soon.

For my pet

Dear God, bless my pet
whose name is ....
As your helper in creation
    make me remember my job
        is to feed and care for ....

Thank you that my pet brings me so much joy
as it returns my love and shares my play.

Help people throughout the world
    to care for all your animals
as we share this planet home together.

For my school

Dear God, bless my school.
I have lots of friends in my class
    and there is much to learn from my teachers.

Make our school a place where
    everyone is respected,
    truth is upheld,
    discovery is encouraged
and where we celebrate the achievements of all.

So dear God, bless my school today.

For my church

Lord Jesus, your church is the place
    where your disciples come to worship you
    and to learn how to serve you.

Please bless my church, its leaders and its people.

Help us to hear the Good News of your love
    and to receive your life-giving power.
Then we will go out with joy
    to make you known in all the world.

For my country

Lord of every nation,
thank you for the country to which I belong;
    make it a caring place in which to live.

Help us to respect the different cultures in our land
    and to live together in harmony.

Bless our leaders that they will guide us
    into ways of justice and peace.
Bless our people that we might play our part
    in making your world a better place.

MY PRAYERS AT SPECIAL TIMES

On my birthday

Creator God,
    It's my birthday today!
Everyone makes me feel so special
    and I like being one year older.

Thank you for
    the gift of my life
and all the love
    shown to me.

As I grow up, shape and guide me
    to be the person
        you and I want me to be.
So make this a great day,
    as I share my joy with family and friends.

Hurray for holidays

Hurray for holidays! I like school,
   but I like holidays even more.

Dear God, you set apart times for rest and holiday
   so your people will not be tired-out through work.
Bless our holidays and make them times
   when we are refreshed and relaxed;
   when we can share play and sport
      with family and friends;
   when we can find space
      to listen to your voice and the song of creation.

Then, renewed, we can return to school
   with a clear mind and a joyful heart.

Christmas is here again

Jesus, Christmas was your birthday
and I want to celebrate it with you.
Thank you for sharing our world
and showing us how to live to the full.

Help me to share your love with others
as I choose the presents
   I give to family and friends.

At Christmas

May the joy of the angels,
    the faith of the shepherds
    and the courage of the wise men
be your gifts to us
    as we join in worship
        on the festival of your birth.

Sadness and joy at Easter

Jesus our Saviour, we remember
 that this was a special week for you –
  from Palm Sunday to Easter Day.
Help us to follow your journey
 from the shouts of praise to the cries of pain
and then to your new greeting of peace at Easter.

Thank you for bringing us forgiveness by your Cross,
and new life and undying hope by your rising again.

This Easter, help me
to be among those disciples
 who believe in you
  and commit their lives to you
   for the journey to heaven.

First steps in faith

Lord Jesus, I am so excited
    as I take this step of faith
        and receive you into my heart
at my ....
    (Baptism, First Communion, Confirmation)

Give me your Spirit of joy and peace,
    and strength and courage
        to keep my promises
            to follow you faithfully for ever.

Bless me and all in my church
    as we worship and serve you,
        and witness to your love
           in everything we do,
    through your gifts of grace.

When I am sick

Healing God, I am sick
    and I feel awful.
I am so sick that I am missing ....
    and it's not fair!

But hang on,
    lots of people get sick
        and lots of people get well again,
    so turn my thoughts to your loving care for me,
        well or sick.

Set me on the pathway to health.
    Give me your healing strength;
        help me know that I am cared for;
    and keep me patient
        to give my body time to heal.

Thank you Jesus for hearing my prayer
    and making me calm again.

When someone I love has died

Comforting God, I am so sad,
    and the tears won't stop
        because ……………………… has died.
I loved ……………………… so much.

What happens now?
Where will they take ………………………?
Help me to ask my questions with care
    and to listen patiently to the answers
        that I don't always understand.

The older people talk of 'resurrection'.
I pray that this means that ………………………
    will always be in your presence
        in a new kind of life.
That is what Jesus promised us
    when he too died and went into heaven.

As I keep remembering ………………………
    may *she/he* rest
        in the peace of your love.

We were special friends

Dear God, ... was my special friend,
but now *she/he* does not want to play with me any more.

I'm sad if I have hurt *her/him*,
    and I will try to say sorry.

    Maybe we can be friends again.

Please help me find good friends,
    and teach me to be a friend
        who listens
        and cares
        and understands
        and laughs
    when we are together as friends.

When I am hurt by others

Dear God, ... hurt me today.
   I feel sad because I thought we were friends.
Now I feel so alone. Some of the others in my class
   were not too nice to me as well.

Please comfort me and direct me –
   guide me how to tell a grown up
      (family member/teacher/friend).
Though it is hard,
   I pray for those who hurt me.
If part of it was my fault,
   I am sorry and will tell them so tomorrow.
If they are just being bullies, then give me
   courage to stand up for myself,
   guidance to help them change
   and love in my heart
      to work for harmony.

Going away on my own

Loving God, I am going away on my own
    and I am very excited,
        but just a little bit afraid too.
Our families have made all the plans
    and I think it will be fun –
        but it is just different on your own.

    Dear God, help me to remember my family loves me
        wherever I am
    and that your love and care is everywhere.
        With that in mind I can go
            with a hop and a skip and a prayer.

I feel uncomfortable

Caring God, I do not feel comfortable
    when I am with ....
and no one else is there.

Help me to find ways to keep my distance
    and to seek the company of others.

I ask you to guide me to an adult whom I can trust
    so that I can tell them about this.
I want to explain that I am unhappy
    and uncertain about what to do.

Loving God,
    please help me find support .
        and keep me safe from harm.

Squabbles in our family

Lord Jesus, I need your help.
    You knew what to do
        when there were squabbles.
In our family the laughter is gone
    and we are left in an awful mess.
I keep listening to the squabbles
    between .... and ....
I am frightened! It is tearing us apart
    and home is not the same.
Let your Spirit of loving replace their spirit of fighting.

    Don't let this break my heart;
        keep me loving,
        keep me strong,
        keep me kind and helpful.
    Above all, keep me near to your sure love
        and then I will not be so frightened.

Watching the family split up

Loving Lord Jesus, I don't know how to say this
    but my family is dividing,
    and Mum and Dad tell us
        they don't want
            to live together any more.

There is horrible talk about where we kids will live.
I hear about getting lawyers
    to agree about who gets the house
        and all sorts of other stuff
            I don't quite understand.
What can I do to make a difference?

I pray that you will forgive us all
    and guide us into the best plan for everybody.

In this time of breaking up,
    Jesus stay very close to me.
Help me to draw on your love,
    so that my love will continue
    for each member of the family
    my Mum, my Dad and my ....
Then in the circle of your love,
    wherever we are,
    we will not be far apart.

Being part of a new family

Dear God, something new has happened.
My *parent* has found a new partner
    and they seem so happy together.
So we are on the move again,
because there are children in the other family too.

It will be hard to share my *Mum/Dad* with others
    in a larger family
and I will have to get along with new *brothers/sisters*.
Help me to take my place in this new plan
    and to be loving and caring to all,
        knowing that my *Mum/Dad* will always
            have a special love for me.

A note from the authors

We offer our thanks to all those who helped to inspire this book and bring it to publication.

We are grateful to our two granddaughters and their generation who bring us new energy and hope for the future.

We were encouraged to proceed by the Editor and staff at Veritas Publications Ltd in Dublin, Ireland, and by our distributors in Australia. Olivia Jackson-Mee immediately responded to our request to provide the illustrations and she has done a wonderful job. Her artistic ability grows with each passing year. We are grateful to Helen Fairs, Graphic Designer at GEON our printers, for taking such care in setting the illustrations and the text on each page.

The Reverend Jo Kelly-Moore, the Vicar of St Aidan's, Remuera, and the Parish Vestry gave us the go-ahead to use accumulated funds from the sale of the previous books to launch this addition to the series. We had the advice of Annette Woodhead of St Joseph's School, Takapuna, in reviewing the text and signalling that the topics and word level for the prayers were right for the focus age group. Finally we give thanks to God for the 'miracles' of prayer we have witnessed as we see families and young people grow in their relationship with God and experience real outcomes in response to their intercessions.

As a new part of our plan to help children pray, we invite them to join THE PRAYER KIDS' CLUB, registering by email their name and email address to prayer.kids@staidans.co.nz.

Check out the Club on the website at www.staidans.co.nz for the latest news about prayer and to keep up with the new prayers for your age group posted regularly on that site. Every blessing to you all as you use these prayers.

+ Peter and Rosemary Atkins, St Heliers, Auckland
St Francis Day, October 2007